Christopher Columbus

Minna Lacey

Illustrated by David Cuzik

Series editor: Lesley Sims
Designed by Russell Punter
and Natacha Goransky

First published in 2004 by Usborne Publishing Ltd.,
Usborne House, 83-85 Saffron Hill, London
EC1N 8RT, England.
www.usborne.com

Printed in Spain. UE.
First published in America in 2005.

Contents

Chapter 1

Going to sea

Christopher Columbus longed to go to sea. He thought about it all day and dreamed of it all night. Living near the busy port of Genoa, in Italy, he loved watching ships arrive from far away places, packed with precious silks and spices. He would gaze at the busy, shouting merchants, the sailors and sea captains with a determined look on his face. One day, he'd be among them.

His father ran a
weaving business
and expected
Columbus to join him.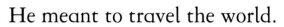
But his son had other ideas.
He meant to travel the world.

When he was 14, he joined a
merchant ship that carried goods to
sell in ports all over the Mediterranean.

Columbus wanted to learn all he
could about the sea. When he wasn't
scrambling up ropes or scrubbing
decks, he was teaching himself to read
and looking at great charts of the
ocean. He experimented with using a

compass and
learned to
plot the
ship's
position.

Then, when he was 26, everything
changed. Columbus was sailing on a
ship near the coast of Portugal when
French warships fired at the crew.

Columbus jumped into the sea
and grabbed hold of a floating oar.
Clinging on tightly, he drifted until
he came ashore near Lisbon, the
capital of Portugal.

The year was 1477 and Portugal
was flourishing from trade with newly
discovered lands along the coast
of Africa.

When Columbus arrived in Lisbon he was amazed by the vast port, bursting with ships. "This is the place for a sailor to be!" he thought.

From Lisbon he joined merchant ships sailing to distant corners of the Atlantic: to Britain and Iceland in the north, the Azores to the west and the Canary Islands and Africa to the south.

When he wasn't at sea, Columbus stayed in Lisbon, earning money by making and selling maps. One day, he met Doña Felipa, the daughter of a nobleman, and fell deeply in love.

Soon they were married with a son, Diego. It looked as if Columbus would be a settled family man. Rather than explore new countries, he provided maps for other voyagers.

When Diego was still young, Doña Felipa died. With only a small child for company, Columbus grew restless again. His longing for adventure increased when a fellow map-maker started talking about a great explorer named Marco Polo.

Marco Polo visited some amazing places!

Really? Tell me more...

"Look!" said his friend, showing Columbus a book written by Marco Polo two hundred years before.

"Marco Polo visited the Indies," raved his friend. "He found China and Japan and saw the most incredible things."

"Such as?" Columbus prompted, excitedly.

"Oh, palaces with roofs of solid gold... Markets bursting with rare spices and fine silks..."

"It sounds fantastic!" Columbus replied. "I have to see these places..."

Anyone brave enough to set out on the long journey to the Indies and Asia went overland, following the Silk Route. But, for many explorers, the topic of the moment was finding a quicker way by sea – and the King of Portugal, John II, was keen to encourage them.

Dozens of men were seeking money and the royal blessing to find a sea route to the Indies. Without exception, they planned to sail East. Columbus, who was sure that the world was round, had a different idea.

"Wouldn't it be quicker to sail in the opposite direction?" he wondered. After studying endless maps, charts and books on geography, he was convinced.

"I'll beat them all and reach the Indies by sailing West!" he declared.

Chapter 2

A royal request

Columbus was sure it would only take him a week or so to reach the Indies if he sailed west. The problem was – though Columbus didn't know it – all his maps showed the world much smaller than it really was. And not one showed that there was a huge continent and vast ocean between Europe and Asia.

Columbus needed money and royal support for his expedition. So he

packed his maps and
went to see King John.

Having
explained
his plans,
Columbus
looked at
the king
anxiously.

Your majesty.

"Will you pay for my
trip, sire?" he asked.

The king looked at his advisers, but
they shook their heads in unison.

"He has all his calculations wrong,
your majesty," said one.

"He's crazy," said another. "He's
planning to go the wrong way!"

The king smiled at Columbus.

"No!" he said. "Next!"

Columbus went straight to Spain,

Portugal's biggest rival, taking Diego with him. Leaving his son with some friars at a monastery, he hurried to the palace and requested an audience with King Ferdinand and Queen Isabella.

"Will you pay for a voyage west to the Indies?" he asked. At first, they refused as well.

But Columbus kept asking, again and again. Queen Isabella was very impressed with his determination.

"This is our chance to get even with Portugal," she pointed out to her advisers. After more discussions, they finally agreed to back Columbus and made him a Captain General.

Delighted, he set to work at once, preparing three small ships for his voyage at the Spanish port of Palos.

The first ship, the *Santa María*, was the largest and slowest of the three...

the second was small and fast and named the *Niña*...

and the third was the *Pinta*.

Proudly, Columbus put up a notice about his trip by the port. But finding a crew to sail with a stranger into unknown waters was not so easy.

A crowd of sailors gathered to read the notice, but no one wanted to sign up. Many feared the Atlantic. They had no idea how far it really stretched.

"It's a death trip," one man muttered. The group nodded in agreement.

"I've always heard the Earth is flat," said a second sailor. "And who knows where it ends? If you sail too far across it, you'll fall off the edge of the world."

It looked as if Columbus' trip was doomed. Seeing his difficulties, the Spanish court offered all crew members higher wages. They even offered to free any prisoner who would help make up the numbers. Still no one came forward.

Just as Columbus was beginning to despair, Martín Pinzón – one of the most admired sailors in Palos – decided to join him. Pinzón was equally suspicious of Columbus' plan, but he couldn't resist the promise of gold from the king

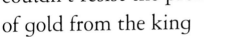

My name is Martín Pinzón.

and queen, not to mention a share in the profits if the trip succeeded.

Columbus made Pinzón captain of the *Pinta* and he persuaded Pinzón's brother, Vincente, to captain the *Niña*. Columbus had already decided to lead the flag ship, the *Santa María*, himself.

As soon as word spread that the famous Pinzón brothers were sailing, plenty of sailors rushed to join.

Columbus was pleased that his voyage could start but, at the same time, he felt uneasy. Martín Pinzón had strong ideas of his own and he was popular with his crew. Would Columbus be able to make him follow orders?

Chapter 3

The first voyage

Even though Columbus was confident it would be a short trip, he didn't want to take any chances. The ships were packed with enough supplies to last a year. Sailors loaded on barrels of water and wine, huge crates of sea biscuits, salted beef and cod, and large sacks bulging with flour, rice, lentils, olives and beans.

Just before dawn on August 3rd, 1492, the three ships set sail.

After only a couple of days at sea, the *Santa María* was lagging behind the two faster ships.

"Those Pinzón brothers are going to get there first," Columbus grumbled.

Why are they always ahead?

On the third day, the rudder broke on the *Pinta*. Columbus still wasn't happy.

"They've done it on purpose to delay us," he complained.

The ships had to stop off in the Canary Islands for repairs, but it meant the sailors could stock up with water and firewood – and some of the local cheeses. On September 6th they were ready again.

"The first to see land wins a year's pay and a coat of silk from Queen Isabella," Columbus roared to his men.

Strong winds took the ships west at full speed. The hulls were packed so heavily, there was nowhere for the sailors to sleep at night but on the equally crowded decks. And, when the weather was stormy, waves crashed over the sides.

Zzzzz...

The further
away from
Spain they
sailed,
the more
each sailor
wondered if
he would ever see

home again. Many sang songs to keep
their spirits up.

Three weeks went by. Then, one
morning, Pinzón thought he glimpsed
land. His weary crew couldn't contain
their excitement.

"We did it! At last!" they cried with
relief. But what looked like land turned
out to be nothing more than low clouds
on the horizon.

On and on they sailed, the sailors
desperate to see land. Columbus

couldn't blame them for being fed up. The biscuits were full of weevils and the meat was crawling with maggots.

From the day they set off, he had been careful to write notes about the voyage in the ship's log. But he kept two copies. One – in Portuguese – he showed his men. The other he wrote in Italian, his first language, and kept it hidden. The Portuguese log had shorter distances, as in those days Portuguese and Italian miles were different lengths.

When historians later compared the two logs, they wondered if Columbus had been trying to trick his men into thinking they had sailed less far. No one knows for sure – though a good captain had to think of ways to keep his men calm on such long voyages.

What was certain was that, after more than a month at sea, the sailors were growing restless. Some even talked of mutiny.

"The captain's lost," said one.

"Let's hurl him overboard," suggested another.

But before they could carry out their threat, something amazing happened.

Chapter 4

Land ahoy!

Just as Columbus himself was about to give up on the whole idea and turn back, a sailor on the *Pinta* spotted land. At once, Martín Pinzón ordered a cannon to be fired to alert the ships.

Sure enough, there in the distance was a golden beach. Taking out his log, Columbus recorded the date in a shaky hand: October 12th, 1492.

They had reached an unknown island of the Bahamas, part of the

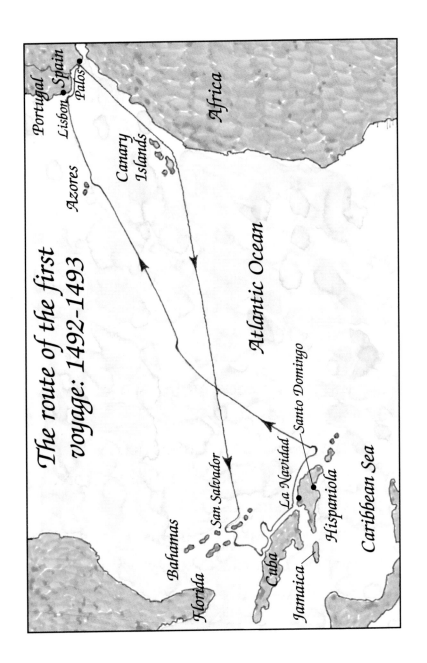

The route of the first voyage: 1492–1493

American continent. But Columbus was convinced they'd landed in the Indies, near Japan.

Land ahoy!

I didn't think the Indies would look like this...

The sailor on the *Pinta* was keen to claim Isabella's reward.

"Sorry," Columbus announced. "I actually spotted land the night before. The reward is mine."

Martín Pinzón was furious when he heard that, though he said nothing.

Together with his fellow captains, Columbus rowed ashore. Striding up

the beach, he hammered a wooden
cross into the sand and hoisted the
three ships' flags.

"I name this new land San Salvador,"
announced Columbus, "and claim it
for Spain and Queen Isabella! And
you can call me Admiral from now
on," he added.

The Tainos, the people who lived on
San Salvador, heard the commotion
and came out of their huts to see
what was going on. Columbus was
astonished to see they wore few clothes.

The Tainos were equally amazed by the Spaniards' ships. They were convinced Columbus had come down from the sky.

He's naked!

Is he a god?

Some of the islanders dragged out canoes and paddled across to the Spanish ships, bringing gifts of spears, parrots, feathers, cotton and dried leaves. In return, the Spanish sailors gave them blue glass beads, bells and red caps – which were greatly admired by the Tainos.

Thrilled with his
success, Columbus decided to
sail on in search of Japan or China. He
soon reached another large island.

"Maybe this is Japan," he said to his
men. In fact, though he didn't know it,
they'd landed on Cuba.

Columbus was full of wonder at
everything he saw, but nothing
compared to the gold and riches he
had expected to find in the East.

Meanwhile, the Spanish sailors were
happy to explore. They discovered the
islanders slept in hanging beds called

hammocks and tasted pineapple
and peppers for the first time.

They watched, amazed, as the
Tainos cooked giant lizards on a grill
they called a barbecue...

...and they gasped when
the islanders put bunches
of smoking leaves to
their lips. The Spaniards
had never seen tobacco before.

But Martín Pinzón was growing
impatient.

"Where's all the gold you said we
would find?" he demanded. "Everyone
should follow me to find gold."

"No," Columbus said angrily. "We must stay together."

Pinzón had had enough. Ignoring Columbus, he ordered his crew back on board and sailed the *Pinta* away.

"Traitor!" Columbus yelled in fury. But there was nothing he could do. Now there were only two ships left.

In December, Columbus found a new island the natives called Haiti. It reminded him of Spain, so he called it La Isla Española (the Spanish Island), or Hispaniola, for short.

On Christmas Eve, sailors on the *Santa María* were resting close to Hispaniola. The sea was completely calm and a young cabin boy was left in charge of the helm. But, just after midnight, the ship crashed into a coral reef.

"Help! We've hit rocks," the boy shouted, running around in a panic.

Christmas morning saw the sailors desperately unloading goods from the wrecked *Santa María*. Local villagers paddled out in canoes to help.

With everything safe on land, the villagers invited the sailors to a feast. After serving plates piled high with grilled fish and mashed yucca plant, they presented the crew with necklaces and masks made of gold.

Columbus was overwhelmed by their kindness. "We'll build a fort here," he decided, ordering the men to use timber from the wrecked *Santa María*. And he named it La Navidad, "Christmas" in Spanish.

But it was too risky to stay on and explore further with just one ship. It was time to go home. Some sailors offered to stay in Navidad to defend the new fort.

"I'll be back soon with more ships and supplies," Columbus promised.

Chapter 5

Triumphant return

Four months after he'd left Spain, Columbus set sail for home. Later that same morning, a sailor at the top of the mast saw another ship in the distance.

"Ship ahoy!" he shouted. It was the *Pinta*. Before long, the two ships were anchored side by side.

As Columbus waited, Martín Pinzón came aboard the *Niña* and made excuses for sailing off on his own.

Despite their differences, Columbus was pleased to have company and the ships set off for Spain together. But, only a few days later, a terrible storm blew up. The rain lashed down and howling winds drove the *Pinta* out of sight.

Columbus didn't care. His only worry now was getting back to Spain before Pinzón. But the *Niña* was badly battered by the storm, and he feared she would sink before they reached home. So, he wrote a letter to the Spanish court describing all the things they had discovered. Sealing his letter in a barrel, he threw it overboard.

The storm raged on and the winds drove the ship off course.

When Columbus finally sailed into the port of Palos, it was to a hero's welcome. Cheering crowds rushed to the jetty with drums beating and trumpets blaring.

Pinzón arrived at Palos only a few hours later. His ship had actually reached Spain first, landing higher up the coast, but the king and queen had refused to see him without Columbus.

Worse still, Pinzón had grown sick on the journey back and he was in a bad way. He survived just long enough to see Columbus win all the glory, then he died.

Columbus went to meet Ferdinand

and Isabella at the court in Barcelona. His arrival was sensational. The king and queen were astounded by his stories and could only gaze in wonder at the incredible things he had brought back.

There were vibrant green parrots...

...strange fruits and vegetables, plus gold, cotton and tobacco – not to mention several scantily-clad Tainos.

Columbus was heaped with grand new titles – Admiral of the Sea, Governor of the Indies – and given other rewards on top, including his own coat of arms. His story of the trip was rushed into print and immediately retold in several languages.

King Ferdinand and Queen Isabella were so thrilled with his triumph, Columbus hardly had time to draw breath, before they gave him money for a second voyage, with a huge fleet.

Chapter 6

The battle for Hispaniola

Columbus sailed back across the Atlantic in September 1493 with 17 ships loaded with supplies, horses and 1,200 very excited men. Among them were priests who wanted to spread Christianity, craftsmen to build houses in the new lands, and soldiers and noblemen eager for riches.

First, they sailed to Navidad to meet up with the men who had stayed behind. A terrible sight greeted them.

The fort lay in ruins and
every single man had
been killed.

Who can have
done this?

Columbus was distraught but,
pulling himself together, he gathered
his new crew and chose a place for a
second settlement, down the coast.

"I name this settlement Isabella, after
our glorious queen," he declared. The
place was a bad choice. Isabella was
infested with mosquitoes and hundreds
of Spaniards caught a deadly fever.

Meanwhile, the Tainos were suffering too, catching smallpox and measles from the Europeans and dying in their thousands.

Columbus wasn't going to let dying men stop him. He had discovered small amounts of gold on Hispaniola and was desperate to find more. But he had hardly begun exploring nearby islands, when he too fell sick and was forced to turn back. He arrived to find Hispaniola in chaos.

Angry at the lack of gold and the rapidly spreading fever, the settlers had started to fight among themselves. Bands of men were stealing from the Tainos, and the Tainos were beginning to fight back.

Then terrible news reached Columbus. The local leaders had had enough and were gathering a vast army, thousands strong, to attack him.

Bluntly, Columbus broke the news to his men. "We'll have to fight them," he said. "Now, I know we only have two hundred soldiers, but we can still win any battle. What good are their spears against our swords and guns?" As the Spaniards began to mutter to each other, he added, "And don't forget we have horses. The Tainos are on foot."

With a determined scowl, Columbus led his soldiers to face the Taino army. On his word, the Spaniards fired their guns and charged. When the Tainos saw the Spaniards riding on horseback, they were terrified. They had never even seen horses before.

Some ran, though many fought back bravely. But the Spaniards overpowered them all and hundreds of Tainos were killed or taken prisoner.

The Spaniards didn't give up until they had conquered the entire island. After numerous battles, they took control, forcing the Tainos to bring them regular payments of gold.

Some Spanish settlers, shocked by this lack of order and the harsh treatment of the Tainos, wrote letters to Ferdinand and Isabella complaining about Columbus.

Columbus decided to return to Spain to defend himself.

Chapter 7

Fall from glory

When he returned, Columbus went straight to the court, where he presented the king and queen with another fine array of gifts. Isabella was thrilled but many in the court knew all was not well in the new territories. Some advisers even began to doubt that Columbus had found the Indies as he claimed.

It was to be nearly two years before Columbus set sail again. In May 1498, he left for his third voyage across the Atlantic. But, during the trip, the wind suddenly dropped and his ships lay becalmed under a hot July sun.

The heatwave lasted for eight days. Water began to run out, the ship's wine turned to vinegar and many sailors grew sick.

Finally, the wind started to blow again and, as the ships moved at last, Columbus sighted land – an island with three sloping hills. Grateful he had reached land alive, and sure it was an act of God, he named the island Trinidad, after the Holy Trinity.

But, as the ship sailed through a dangerous channel between Trinidad and an unknown mainland, Columbus became aware of a roaring sound. It was terrifying – and growing louder every second. As Columbus and his sailors watched in horror, a giant wave headed straight for the ship. Panic-stricken, they could only watch and wait.

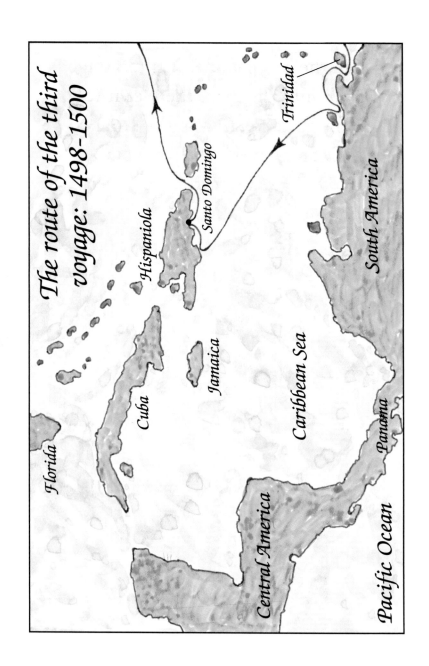

The route of the third
voyage: 1498–1500

Trinidad

Santo Domingo

Hispaniola

South America

Jamaica

Cuba

Caribbean Sea

Florida

Panama

Central America

Pacific Ocean

When the wave came, it lifted the ship high into the air... then let it fall with a mighty crash onto the swirling ocean. Water covered the decks, the ship was battered and the crew were bruised. But, miraculously, they survived.

Undeterred, Columbus continued to explore the coast. Several days later, he reached the mouth of a vast river.

"I've discovered an enormous land, an unknown continent!" he announced with excitement. He had no idea he'd just discovered South America.

But, feeling ill, he sailed to the new capital of Santo Domingo on Hispaniola. There he learned that the Spanish settlers were rebelling against him. As Governor of the Indies, Columbus tried in vain to calm them.

Ships returned to Spain with news of mounting disorder in Hispaniola. In alarm, the Spanish court sent a nobleman, Francisco de Bobadilla, to investigate. When Bobadilla arrived, he decided Columbus was entirely to blame.

Ignoring Columbus' protests, Bobadilla arrested him and shipped him back to Spain in chains.

Ferdinand and Isabella were shocked to see Columbus return in disgrace. They instantly pardoned him, but Columbus never forgot his ordeal. He kept the chains by his bedside for the rest of his life.

Chapter 8

The final voyage

The return from his previous trip had been truly shameful, but Columbus still longed to go back to the new lands. Daily, he pleaded with the Spanish court to let him go, and finally they gave in. In 1502, he set sail on his fourth Atlantic voyage accompanied by four ships. But there was a condition attached.

"Dear Columbus," Isabella had said, in her regal way, "If you go, you are

not to land at Santo Domingo.
Another man is in charge now, and
we want no more trouble."

Columbus had reluctantly agreed,
but, as he sailed near
Hispaniola, the
weather grew
worse.

Even though
officials at the
port in Santo
Domingo could
see his ships were in
danger, they refused to let Columbus
land. He had to shelter as best he could
close by.

The storm became a hurricane that
raged around the ships, tearing the sails
to pieces. Anchors and rigging were lost
and many of the sailors were killed.

By sheer luck, the ships survived. A
Spanish fleet leaving Santo Domingo
was not so lucky. The entire fleet sank,
including the ship carrying Columbus'
arch enemy, Bobadilla.

The storm continued for eighty-eight days. Columbus ignored it and sailed on, through thunder, rain and lightning, exploring the new coastline to Panama and back.

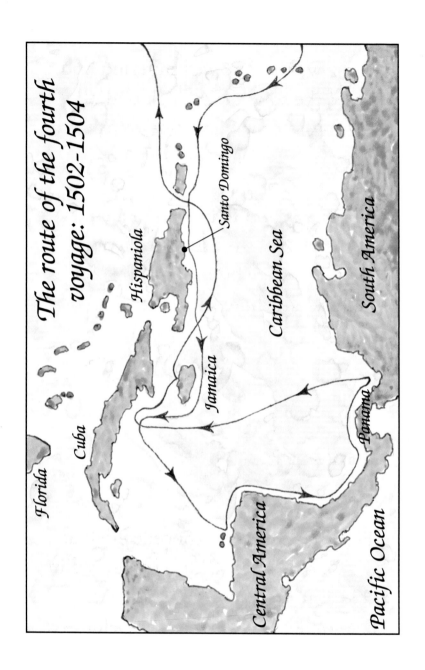

The route of the fourth
voyage: 1502–1504

Florida

Cuba

Hispaniola

Santo Domingo

Jamaica

Caribbean Sea

Panama

Central America

South America

Pacific Ocean

By now, his crew was suffering badly. Half of the sailors were sick and all were infested with lice. The ships were no better off, with woodworm eating away at the timbers.

Two ships had to be abandoned altogether and the other two leaked. The sailors were bailing out day and night, using whatever was handy.

Finally, Columbus conceded defeat. "We'll have to land," he announced in despair. It was a terrible moment. They landed in Jamaica just before the ships fell apart. They were far from any Spanish settlement and in danger of being marooned there forever.

Columbus ordered his men to turn the wood from the wrecked ships into straw-roofed huts. One of his more loyal crewmen decided to take action.

"We can't stay here," he told Columbus. "I'm taking a canoe to Hispaniola to find help."

"It's too dangerous," Columbus replied, but he said it quietly. Both men knew it was their only hope.

He'll never survive the rough crossing.

As the days passed, the sailors left behind grew angry. It was Columbus' fault they were in this mess. Columbus should pay. Soon, over half the men had agreed to replace him as leader.

A fierce battle erupted between the mutineers and those sailors who still supported Columbus. His side won eventually, but Columbus was so tired and sick, he thought he would probably die on the island.

Then, in June 1504, after they had been on Jamaica almost a year, one of the men spotted a dot on the horizon.

"I don't believe it! It's a ship!" he cried, racing down the beach in amazement. Sure enough, their crewmate had returned to rescue them.

Columbus fell to his knees to thank God, tears of joy and relief streaming down his cheeks. Later that year, he finally sailed back to Spain – a sick man. On May 20th 1506, in the town of Valladolid, in Spain, Columbus died at the age of 54.

Even on his deathbed, Columbus was convinced he had discovered the Indies. Never in his wildest dreams did he believe he had really found a new land, a place people would actually name the New World, many thousands of miles from Asia.

Perhaps, if he had realized, America would have been named after him, rather than the navigator Amerigo Vespucci who sailed to America in the early 1500s and recognized a new world when he saw it.

My life at sea

1451 – I was born in Genoa, Italy.

1471 – I am shipwrecked but swim to shore in Portugal. What a city! I start living in Lisbon.

1475 – I marry Doña Felipa Moniz.

1480 – Our son Diego is born.

1484 – I seek support for my voyage to the Indies from King John of Portugal. He refuses me.

1485 – Doña Felipa dies. I seek backing from King Ferdinand and Queen Isabella of Spain.

1492 – At last, Ferdinand and Isabella agree to help. I set sail from Palos, Spain, on the first voyage across the Atlantic... and months later, I have my first sight of the Indies! I land in the Bahamas and discover Cuba and Hispaniola (Haiti). The Santa María is wrecked and we build a fort at La Navidad.

1493 – I return to Spain a hero and am warmly received by the King and Queen in Barcelona. I become Admiral of the Ocean. I set sail from Cadiz on the second Atlantic voyage. I find the fort at Navidad has been destroyed and all the Spanish settlers killed.

1494 – I explore Cuba and Jamaica.

1495 – We fight with the Tainos to take control of Hispaniola.

1496 – I return to Spain.

1498 – I depart from Sanlucar, Spain on my third voyage. I discover Trinidad and the mainland of a new continent. [South America] A gigantic wave nearly sinks the ship. There's a rebellion on Hispaniola.

1500 – The vile Francisco de Bobadilla arrests me and sends me back to Spain in chains. The King and Queen pardon me.

1502 – I depart from Cadiz, Spain on my fourth voyage and am denied shelter from a storm in Santo Domingo. Undeterred, I begin to explore a new coastline. [Central America]

1503 – I am marooned in Jamaica. Diego Mendez canoes to Santo Domingo to seek help. Half the crew mutinies against me. Luckily, my side wins.

1504 – Diego Mendez brings a ship to rescue us. I return to Spain, a sick man.

Christopher Columbus died at Valladolid in Spain on May 20th 1506.